With Assistance from:

Wendi Newman

Ophilia Mandara

Woody:

My Journey through Joy, Grief, and Healing with a Dog

I'd like to say that my journey with Woody and his sudden passing is over. I've learned that it's not. I find things changing every day. He still comes to visit. This true story is about an animal that so affected my life that I thought I would never recover, but I am, little by little. This is a nontraditional book in that I am writing as things happened to me. I wish I could organize this document a little better, but the growth I experienced was in huge spurts and then nothing. Everything in here is true and reported to the best of my ability. I am so grateful to my wife Wendi Newman, to whom I can never show my gratitude enough.

This life event has truly been that - a life event. It has changed me in so many ways. I know so much more about myself and how I interact with the world and others. I hope sharing my pain and growth will also help the reader. Even though my doctors all told me I would get through it, it was hard to believe there is life after grief.

To Woody, who changed my life in so many ways. To my wife Wendi Newman, who has stuck by me. Her understanding and compassion for animals is boundless. To Dr. Eliot Light, for his wisdom, understanding, and compassion, to Dr. John Paul Beaudoin, who helped me understand my feelings, and to Ophilia Mandara of Planetary Dreams, who helped me understand my dreams and empowered me with a new way of living. I can't thank you all enough.

Prologue

I wasn't a pet person when I met my wife in 1982. She had a parrot that hated me, and I still bear scars on one finger from a bad bite. He passed away after about a year. We got another parrot, and she died in our hands after the Northridge earthquake. The stress was too much for her.

We got our first Great Dane a year before we moved to Monterey Bay, and he was the beginning of my journey with dogs. After him, we had six more before we got Woody. Great Danes don't have long life spans, and we lost all but one before eight years. All of these losses were difficult in the moment, but all had illness or disease as the reason for their passing. I seemed to be able to process those losses and move on to the next dog.

Then came Woody.

There are four voices in this book: myself, Dream Richard, Wendi, and Ophilia Mandara.

Table of Contents

Section One Joy and Grief

Chapter 1

We were sitting in our front room one night, and Wendi was looking at Facebook. I saw her staring at a post. She looked over at me and said, "This puppy just grabs my heart." When I looked at the picture, I wasn't sure it was for us, but she was. We began a conversation with the breeder. The Great Dane puppy had very unusual markings; he was a show stopper. The puppy was about nine hundred miles away from us.

We had once shipped a puppy from the East Coast. I was on the East Coast and thought I'd pick him up and fly with him, but that didn't work out. The flight from Boston to San Francisco was over six hours. We had a headwind, and it was one of the roughest flights I'd ever been on. I'm an experienced flyer (with over 750,00 miles in the air), but this one was rough. The puppy, who we named Sherman, was on a different plane an hour behind me.

Nine-and-a-half-week-old Sherman was alone and most likely scared out of his mind. The poor little guy was covered in poop and exhausted after this disorienting flight. He slept on the back seat of our van all the way home, including during a flat tire repair on Highway 101 - he never moved.

Sherman was an interesting pup. He was very loving but also very reactive to dogs.

Wendi's words.

Sherman came to us many years before I understood behavior. I was just an experienced dog owner, not even an amateur trainer. I know now the term "reactivity" in dogs is what we humans would term an overreaction to other animals, people, moving objects, etc. Sometimes, it is lights or shadows, a simple leaf blowing down the street, sounds, or anything we think of as a normal event but which an animal sees as a contrast, so to speak, in the environment. The reasons for it are often complex, but fearfulness, lack of socialization, anxiety, physiological problems, and genetics can all contribute to it.

We noticed this right away in him at five months old and knew we had a problem we needed to address. Sherman grew into a one-hundred-and-fifty-pound dog, and his lunging and barking reactions were difficult to handle. Wendi looked for help and couldn't find anybody at that time who even knew the basics of how to help us. Most of the suggestions were corrective obedience, and she knew she needed to forge a new pathway with him.

Wendi changed careers. She threw herself into learning about dog behavior. She studied at Marin Humane, which meant a trip of over two hundred miles every weekend for two years. She received her first certification, left her university job as a researcher, and went to work for a large shelter near us.

Sherman adored her, and one day, they were walking together on the trail that runs along the Pacific Ocean. A female deer that had just birthed her baby charged at them as they were walking. Sherman calmly stepped between her and the deer and protected her. There was no fight; the deer rammed into him and then ran off. He remained calm during the whole incident, as if he really understood what needed to be done. That was protection! With all the reactivity he had displayed in his life, this was astounding. He was very special.

Sherman was her motivation to learn about behavior and she flourished. He taught us so much and became the guiding light for helping dogs. His behavior improved to the point people observing him out on walks never knew he was reactive. He was a wonderful, loving, loyal companion.

Like everything Wendi does, she excels at dog behavior.

Wendi has now been a certified dog behavior consultant for many years and has a Bachelor of Science degree and many behavior certifications. She works with people and their dogs, and with shelter dogs. Her work is perfect for her. She can be consumed by it and often has to work on very difficult behavioral problems. She has risen to the top of her field and has clients from around the United States. This is all thanks to an amazing Sherman.

Sherman was able to mentor our next fabulous Dane, Delta. It was one of the best things we ever did for him. They simply adored each other! When Sherm passed, we got

Shelby, who was the sweetest, kindest boy. Delta and Shelby had many lovely years together. Shelby left us, and then, right at the end of Delta's life with us, Faith appeared. She was about a year and a half old when we first saw Woody's picture.

I knew that this new puppy was coming and I would not ship him, so we waited until our schedules would allow us a three-day trip north.

Faith couldn't wait for her new brother to arrive.

Chapter 2

We drove from 6 that morning till 9 that night. It was a beautiful drive. California 5 can be mind-numbing, but I had made the drive before. Northern California into Southern Oregon is some of the most breathtaking scenery on the planet. We collapsed into our room at the hotel, and after hot baths, we had a microwave dinner at the hotel gift shop. It was the first time in about six years that Wendi and I had traveled together; I was grateful for the road time with her. Our anticipation for the next day was high and we slept well.

We were up at 6 am, full of anticipation for the day ahead. We got gas and breakfast and headed to the breeder at 8 am. We walked in, and there he was. It took about an hour to do all the paperwork and prepare the car for the trip home. We rolled south about 9 and drove to Portland to stop and see an old friend and give Woody (we hadn't  chosen a name yet) a break. Our first picture of him was in our friend's backyard.

He was a great traveler. We had a crate in the back seat with a lot of blankets. When we started to drive, he went to sleep. When we stopped for a pee break, he would do his business and fall back asleep. You can see by his markings that he was special.

We spent the night in a small town in the redwoods. The restaurant was closed, and the only food was ice cream sandwiches, so I went out to find dinner for us while Wendi stayed with the boy. The town was quite a place, and I got lost trying to find food. I ended up in somebody's driveway, and to my shock, they came out on the porch with a shotgun. I got out of there fast and found a deli in a gas station that had sandwiches. I was glad to get back to Wendi and the pup. It wasn't the greatest place to stay, but it was a bed, it was safe, and we left early the next morning for Monterey and arrived about 5 that night.

We introduced him to his new sister Faith; they became great friends almost immediately.

We still didn't have a name, but that came quickly, Woody…not because of the movie Toy Story, but because he reminded us of a big brown, lumbering "woody" surfing station wagon from the 1940s.

We traced his pedigree back fourteen generations to figure out where his brown color came from, a very unique coloring for sure. He melted my heart.

About four months later, I had a total knee replacement, and both dogs were right there, giving me comfort and joy. Woody just looked at me as I was lying there, wondering when we were going to go for a walk. I tried to explain it to him, and I'm sure he understood.

I think it was during my recovery that I realized that he was going to be very special to me. Wendi describes it as a "heart dog," one that is so special, an old soul, and one that reads you like a book. A dog that constantly surprises you with a showing of a deeper understanding when you are feeling bad. That was Woody for me, just as Sherman was Wendi's heart dog. I had no idea how Woody would change mine. He was our 8th Great Dane. When you have pets, you understand the possible sorrow that will inevitably come… we knew the landscape. I had no idea it would be the great unknown.

Chapter 3

This was my second total knee replacement. Both replacements were very successful, but I found out on the first one that physical therapy was the most critical thing I could do. Woody became a big part of that.

Faith is Wendi's dog; she goes to work with her and helps calm shelter dogs, and she doesn't like to walk with me. Woody was much different. I got a leash, and he was ready to go. We spent a lot of time socializing with both dogs, meeting and greeting dogs, people, and kids in the forest and at the beach while Woody was young, as we do with all our dogs. Woody and I would go on solo walks when Wendi and Faith were at work.

Woody taught me how to wander. Always before, when I'd walk one of our dogs, I had a direct route in mind. But he and I would go wander. I named a cue for him to get ready: "Let's Wander." Woody was super friendly and would walk up to anyone with a big wag and a smile. He was growing fast, and by the time I felt I was able to control him, he was close to one hundred pounds. For the first couple of months, Wendi and Faith would go with me in case he pulled me off my feet, not to chase something but to meet somebody with that infectious wag. It always brought a smile to the faces of those he greeted. I'll give you a few examples.

We live in a slightly hilly neighborhood. As I grew stronger, the two of us started tackling the hills. One was quite steep, and there was a house being remodeled about halfway up. It was a good place to stop and sniff and take a bit of a break, with chain link fencing surrounding the property. One morning, a carpenter with a tool belt full of tools approached. Instead of reacting and being fearful, Woody just wagged and walked up to him. Woody just let the guy pet him, rub his ears, or do whatever this stranger wanted to do. I asked his name, and he told me it was Dustin. From that point on, when we would leave the house in the morning and go visit Dustin. Somedays, he would come out and love on Woody; other days, we didn't see him, and Woody would stand at the fence and wag until he decided  that his time was better spent elsewhere, and our wander would continue.

Our neighborhood has a middle school close by with lots of kids walking to and from school. We'd often see kids out walking. One amazing encounter was with a big, clumsy, growing boy who was listening to music. He was wearing headphones and not paying attention to where he was walking. His movements were jerky, and Woody alerted to him. Instead of confronting him, Woody leaned into my leg and just watched the boy. The boy looked up and was startled at seeing such a big dog and kind of jumped backward. Woody didn't react and the kid moved on his way.

A couple of days later, we ran into him again during one of our wanders. This time, the boy saw Woody about thirty feet away and smiled. Woody just started to wag, his entire body leaning against me and waiting. The boy walked up, still wearing his headphones, and extended his hand. Woody let him rub his ears and scratch his back. The kid never took his headphones off, but the smile on his face was huge. I remember just standing there and praising and massaging Woody for a long time, giving him so much reinforcement for his wonderful greeting.

I began to understand the lessons he was sharing with me, the lessons of openness and joy. As my knees became stronger, I started extending our walks to different areas of the neighborhood.

There is a tennis court close to our house. It wasn't so much uphill as it was down from our origin point. When we'd walk home, it would give me a much different stretch of my legs. For most of the time, the courts were empty. They were below the level of the sidewalk with some great bushes for sniffing. Woody would spend a little time there reading the pee-mail; then, he would move on. On Tuesday and Thursday, the City allows pickleball on the courts, which were usually packed with groups of people playing. The first time he saw the games in action with the movement and sound, he glanced at it, leaned into my leg, and walked on by.

The second time was much different. He stopped where he had a clear vantage point and watched. He wasn't leaning against me for comfort; he was watching them play. The next time we passed, he stood and wagged. On this occasion, the players noticed him and talked amongst themselves about him. I told them his name, and we stayed about 10 minutes in that particular spot. The next time the players saw him, they shouted out his name. His wag almost shook him off his feet, and we stood for 20 minutes. After that, we could pass by, pause, be greeted by the pickleball folk, wag, and move on. Every time it happened it filled my heart with awe and wonder.

Woody developed puppy habits too; there are two that I'd like to highlight.

As a puppy, he was amused by entry rugs. My office has a set of French doors, and the one that we open has a heat vent in front of it. To Woody's delight, there was a rug there. I think in the span of two or three months, he must have chewed up 10 of them. He was fascinated by the edges; he would play with them as a puppy would, and in an hour or two, he would

12

destroy them. He wasn't destructive in any other way; he just must have thought those rugs were grand.

The other habit is difficult to talk and think about. He was a very early riser (2 am to start), and that became a big part of his life. Wendi started to work with him, and after a few months, he was awake and ready to go at 4 am. It took another month to get him to sleep till 4:15, then we gradually moved him to sleep till 5 am.

We have a small house and an even smaller bedroom. There is only about a foot between the bed and the closet on my side. Every morning, as soon as he woke up, he would come into the room and push his face into mine, making slobbery puppy noises. These blubbering sounds are hard to describe in a book, but I knew he was talking to me and was asking me for food. Damn, I miss that wake-up call. He was always so happy to see me first thing in the morning. I can still hear his tail beating furiously against the bedroom door. I still feel his head on the foot of the bed in the night. After ten and a half months, his presence in my life is still as strong as the day we lost him.

As my legs and knees grew stronger, our walks continued to increase in length. I'd like to relate two stories that affected me deeply. When the events happened, I was sure that Woody and I would go on to do therapy work at some of the elderly facilities in our immediate neighborhood.

On a walk one morning, we encountered an older lady out with her walker. To a growing Great Dane, a walker can appear as an object from outer space, and I was a little nervous. Woody had it handled from the very beginning. He approached her as if it was the most ordinary thing in the world. He let her pet him, and he just stood next to me while we exchanged greetings. I never asked her name, but she told me about how important dogs were in her life. A school bus went by, and he calmly focused his attention on her. He waited perfectly until she said goodbye and went on with her walker and her morning walk, clattering down the street. After that, we saw her several times; she always waved and shared a smile.

About a month later, we had been watching pickleball for about ten minutes, and he decided to move on. Across the street from us was a very bent-over older lady, again pushing a walker up the slight incline. She was just staring at Woody and could not take her eyes off of him. I asked her if she wanted to meet him, and she said, "Yes."

As I was crossing the street, I was wondering if this was a good idea. He was about one hundred and fifteen pounds at the time and pure muscle. If he saw a squirrel, he'd lurch and possibly knock her down. As we approached, the leash was loose; that was the first good sign. When we got across the street, Woody went to her side and ever so softly leaned into her while she rubbed his head. He stayed like that for over five minutes, and while she told me stories of all the dogs in her life, he was the perfect boy. As we parted, I told myself he might be the best therapy dog ever. After that day, we never saw her again, although we kept a pretty regular routine. Woody had brought so much joy to her.

Chapter 4

Changes

Great Danes grow until about eighteen months or so, and it's critical to allow them this time so that their bones grow correctly. As they grow, their leash training becomes really important. As Woody grew, he became more powerful, and our walks became real workouts for me.

When we walked downtown, we stopped by our auto mechanic, the hardware store, and the coffee house. Woody always greeted everyone with his exuberant wagging; he was so happy to see everyone.

We have a large herd of small deer that live in the neighborhood. After we visited Dustin one morning, we headed up the hill to walk around the park. There were a lot of dogs in the area, and I bet the grass and trees smelled very interesting to Woody. As we passed a workman's trailer that was parked on the street, the clown car opened up, and a herd of about thirty deer ran out about five feet in front of him. He was too powerful for me, and it was either to lose my arm or drop the leash. He was off like a jet in full pursuit. At the end of the street was a busy four-lane highway, and it was the morning rush hour. I was screaming his name at the top of my lungs as he disappeared around the corner. I was listening with terror for the screeching of brakes, but they never came. As soon as he lost sight of me (I swear he had a camera on his tail), he turned around and came back at a full gallop. You could see the testosterone boiling through his face. It took him a long time to calm down, so we just stayed in the park and sniffed before we walked quietly home.

There is one more experience with the "Woody Walk" that I would like to relate. Even though our town has narrow streets, we do have some "Broadway" type streets, which are wide, tree-lined, and four lanes wide but have a twenty-five mph speed limit. Since there is hardly any traffic, people tend to drive kind of fast.

Woody and I were walking at about 7:15 one morning on the street that goes past our Middle School. A little-known fact was that Frank Zappa went to school there for about a year. There is a 3-foot retaining wall between the sidewalk and the elevated grassy front lawn of the school. Woody loved to jump up on the wall and walk alongside me. This time, he jumped up and just took off. I was walking him on an eight-foot leather leash, and there was no holding onto him. He started to run circles on the lawn; then, he started to expand the circles into the street. I was trying to catch him, but it was impossible. I ran into the middle of the street and just started waving my arms in case anybody came speeding down the street. Nobody did, and after the three longest minutes of my life so far, he came back to me. He was panting really hard and wagging his tail. "Wasn't that fun, Dad?" He was King of the Street at that time. I readjusted our walks into areas where I felt safer after that.

Woody was neutered that summer. This is a normal part of raising a dog, and there were no complications.

Wendi's words.

There were some changes we started to see that fall. Woody started to display some inconsistent behavior.

When behavior in an animal starts to change, professionals evaluating that behavior look for events, situations, or illnesses that help us interpret the behavior. The animal might be painful, irritable, or sensitive to environmental surprises. There might be some isolated event, person, or situation causing the animal emotional discomfort. We also look for fear, stress, or anxiety. The animal's physical well-being, training, social life, and familial history create a broader picture. During any evaluation, direct experience with the animal also helps us create behavior modification protocols or referrals to another professional, like a veterinarian, for physical reasons or the need for medication.

What we started to see in Woody was "normal" friendly behavior and, in a split second, aggression toward a person, dog, or situation. These events were unforeseeable and not preceded by anything we could recognize. Woody was not a fearful, anxious, or low-confidence dog; he was a fun, kind, social animal with little stress in his life. He was not protective of Faith or any dog, Richard, or me. But his behavior sharpened our observation and modified activities with him. One thing was consistent - these events started to come closer and closer in time. With each one, it would take Woody time to recover. He had been to the vet and passed check-ups and blood work without issues. At this point, we did not feel he was a danger.

Chapter 5

Two days: Jan 2-3, 2024

The holidays came and went. Both dogs really like Thanksgiving. We had a few people over, and with leftover turkey and friends, we had some very happy puppies. Christmas and New Year were quiet for us.

The rest of this chapter describes aggression and how we lost Woody. If you do not want to read it, go to Chapter 6.

Just after the New Year, we experienced something I never thought possible. What we had experienced outside our home was now inside with us and directed at our core.

Wendi's words.

Woody attacked Faith several times in early January. The last time it was much more difficult to interrupt it, and the intensity of it was different. We were so thankful we were there with them to stop it. Faith was physically fine but was now becoming afraid of him. He was still agitated sometime after this final attack and was not himself. At that moment, I realized something was very wrong with him.

I have seen so many different behaviors through the hundreds of dogs I've evaluated through my work. I got a very sick feeling in the pit of my stomach, knowing this was very serious. I needed more information and guidance.

I loaded Faith into our van to remove her from the house. I drove us to the beach to make some phone calls and figure out what to do. I had a suspicion that he might be experiencing some sort of neurological problem, as I have seen similar behavior like this at work. I called our veterinarians and his two breeders. Everyone was so kind and responded to me immediately.

While she was waiting at the beach, she made her calls. I stayed home with Woody. He had now floated back to more or less being himself, but I do think he was confused at this moment, as I was.

Wendi's words.

Everyone was shocked at what had transpired, and we discussed the possibilities in front of us. We all talked about the "what ifs."

I've worked through this issue with many clients. Unfortunately, some animals can be behaviorally unstable. Some conditions can be managed with medication, training, and a proper physical setup at home to keep everyone safe. When the animal is large, unpredictable, and poses a danger to those around them, other considerations come into play.

In just a few months, we had started to see increasingly

21

unpredictable behaviors. Woody had always been happy to meet and engage with any human or dog. He was always relaxed, and I never worried about introducing him (unless there was a cat or deer nearby!), but I understood that aspect of playfulness in him. He was silly, goofy, and generous in spirit until he started to change.

Wendi's words.

When a situation becomes grave, a multi-dimensional risk assessment is necessary. Risk factors include the size of the animal, predictability and prevention of the behavior, veterinary input, and responsibility to family, friends, neighbors, and community. I am so thankful for my work experience, as it helped me navigate these difficult questions without obscuring what was happening with a river of tears. That would come later.

The first risk we considered was his one hundred and forty pounds and the type of reaction he displayed. It is one thing to react with barking and lunging versus acting violently in the moment. An animal of his size could inflict significant damage. One thing in his favor was the physical character of the bites. At this time, he did not deliver deep, tearing bites, but in each incidence, we were able to grab him instantly before there were serious wounds. Difficulty in interrupting an aggressive event does coincide with highly aroused behavior. And with his size, this level of arousal could be dangerous or fatal to the victim, not to mention the risk of injury we took in trying to stop him.

The second issue was the lack of predictability in his behavior. When people experience aggression with their dogs, they commonly say, "It came out of the blue," meaning they did not see any behavior or body language indicating something was about to happen. There might be only subtle observable signs of impending aggression. In my case, I do know what a dog looks like in this state and can identify the behaviors that show stress, irritation, or motivation to attack someone or something. We observed him very carefully during this time as there was little consistency in his actions.

Prevention of his behavior might include training, veterinary intervention, physical setup, and muzzle training. Woody was well-trained and socialized. There were several times in his life when another male dog would snarl or challenge him, and he would walk away as if to say, "You're weird, dude," and let it go. I was always so proud of this ability in him. When he started to display reactivity, he received regular extra-curricular training. He did very well, but this training did not trigger his more serious behavior, nor did aggressive events coincide with normal training. Aggressive events were managed and triaged, and training was not possible when he was in a highly aroused state. At these times he was not present and able to to think.

Even though Woody was healthy physically, we had no time for a referral to a veterinary specialist. Because of safety issues and the violence he displayed, this factor became less critical. Our veterinarians thought he might be experiencing seizures or even a brain tumor. We never confirmed this diagnosis, but several additional veterinarians months later also thought this was a strong possibility. It was unthinkable at the moment to cause him more emotional stress and pain working through the possible diagnosis while he was not himself. I know there were times he felt disoriented mentally after an event. Richard and I would never allow any animal in our care, much less one we deeply adored, to ever suffer in any way.

I would never have been comfortable rehoming Woody, either. No home was safe for him, and it was not ethical to even return him to his breeders. I felt he had become very unstable, and I would never forgive myself if he hurt them or one of their dogs. He had also never known anyone but us, and this might add to his stress, which might also make him more unstable.

Woody's history was also considered. He had been very gregarious, but his behavior now was unreliable. Who could be at risk for his dangerous behavior - us, Faith, friends, neighbors, and the children and older people who frequent our neighborhood? If he was unpredictable, how would we prevent dangerous behavior? How could we manage his physical space in the home and outside? I did not want him locked in a kennel or wearing a muzzle 24/7.

Faith was now in danger, and now, honestly, possibly us as well. Would this mean his life would be limited to very few outings? How fair was it to him to live a small, very protected life when his life had been so full? How fair was it to Faith to live with a dog she wanted to avoid out of fear? There were no guarantees that we could get him back to where he had been, happy and social. And how responsible was it of us to try to manage all of this within our community? Could we keep everyone, including him, safe?

I have had many dogs in my life, and I have never been worried about safety this way before. But after the events with Faith, I worried about our own family's safety and about Woody's suffering.

In this moment, we witnessed a dog that had lived a very social, happy, calm, solid life that now disintegrated in a very short time into a dog that had fractured our confidence and our hearts. This was a puppy we had raised, nurtured, and profoundly loved.

Our puppy.

Everyone understood he was unstable and relied on my call that his behavior was dangerous. We couldn't trust his behavior at all, either with Faith or with us. He had turned unpredictably ferocious. We had no time for a full veterinary workup without causing him significant anguish. There was only one bleak and crushing answer.

I came home from the beach, left Faith in the van, and Richard and I discussed the phone calls I had made. Richard knew the answer, but let me make the decision. It is a strange feeling to have to judge the behavior and fate of an animal you adore. It took every ounce of strength I had not to break down. I gave my opinion, and we together made the agonizing decision to let him go. I would rather let him pass in peace in our loving arms rather than allow something regrettable to happen. Neither one of us wanted him to hurt anyone or for him to suffer in any way. We loved him too much for that.

Wendi called our vet and made the emergency appointment.

Meanwhile, I was just sitting with Woody in the office. I was in disbelief at his sudden change, and my mind swirled in confusion.

Wendi had called our friends and they knew what was going on. They would sit with Faith while we were gone.

Wendi came back and took Faith out of the van into the backyard. I put Woody's harness on him, and after she was in the yard, we led him out into the van.

We arrived at the vet, and they had a room ready for us. The vet was in tears, and I was a train wreck of emotions but tried not to show them. I tried not to project my feelings so Woody wouldn't pick up on them, but I started to cry. The vet gave him a shot to relax him; they had put blankets on the floor. When he laid down, I was next to him, holding his head and stroking his body, telling him that it was OK to go, that I would be alright, but it was one of the biggest lies I've ever told in my life. Wendi and I continued to pet and talk to him as the drugs took effect. I felt when he took his last breath, and I felt his spirit leave me as well.

I broke down completely. I removed his collar and his tag. I wear it around my neck to this day, along with a piece of jade that resembles the stone we placed for him and his ashes. We left the vet and sat by the ocean for a few minutes to collect ourselves. It was so sudden. I watched all my dreams for him leave my mind. I was confused, but what I knew was that I needed

a drink more than at any time ever in my fifty-three years of drinking. When we went back to the house, our friends hugged us and left. Faith didn't seem to miss him; after all, he had just tried to kill her four hours earlier. I fell apart. I was in shock for the next four to five days. We met our friends at the beach on Sunday so Faith could have a run with their dog. They brought a bottle of good alcohol; we toasted Woody. I couldn't stop crying.

I hadn't slept in five days; I was confronted with horrible nightmares every time I closed my eyes. I drank myself to sleep at night, just to get some rest, but it was no use. I had never experienced such a profound loss in my life. I was a ship without a rudder. I was lost. When his ashes came back, I just couldn't stop crying at the realization.

Chapter 6

January 2024

I was in shock for about five days. I was fortunate that I have been a journal creator all my life and that was what I started to do on the fourth or fifth day. I was also very lucky that I had a great team around me to help. I called my therapist of over twenty years, and we set up some Zoom appointments. I called my general doctor and set up an appointment so he could get a handle on what was going on. I also had my wife, who was grieving herself. Her training in dog behavior and the fact that she had counseled so many others was a help to her, but I was a mess. I was crying all the time, and I felt guilty that I couldn't control my emotions and I felt like a burden to her. On January 9th, she published a deep and moving tribute on Substack called "When Grief Takes the Steering Wheel".[1] As I read it now I am in amazement at her wisdom and clarity at a time when all was black to me. I include it in its entirety here:

Wendi's words...

----

[1]https://raisingfaith.substack.com?utm_source=navbar&utm_medium=web; January 9th, 2004

This column will be a little different.

Raising Faith started when Faith was just a baby. I thought I would write about her growing up and the training we would do and hoped that would be interesting for others. And then Woody came, and my mission expanded to include both dogs. So much of having a pet is about relationships, joy, the love of caring for, nurturing, and growing older with them. We cherish the time we are granted with them until that time runs out.

Time ran out for my family this week. We lost Woody.

I cannot write about this last week yet. Woody was ill, and it caught up with him quickly. One of the promises I make to every animal in my care is that they will never suffer. As soon as we see it, we let them go. And so it was for Woody.

While the details are still too visceral for me, what I would like to write about is grief and the grieving process. If this is too raw or something you do not want to read, stop here.

This newsletter was always meant to be about life. Never in my wildest thoughts did I ever think I would write about being absorbed by grief. Everyone deals with it in their own, very personal way. This writing will be about me. Writing helps me express my feelings. Richard is experiencing this is his own way and will share when he is ready.

There are basically five basic stages of grief: shock and

denial, anger, bargaining, depression, acceptance, and hope. The process of grieving and mourning is also fluid. One can jump through different stages in one day or go to one stage, jump back to another, and re-experience the same stage again repeatedly. From what I've read, the most crucial part is fluidity. The grieving process is alive and responsive to our emotions, as if in a big feedback loop.

My own journey has been shock, then right to bargaining and depression. I'm not angry or in denial, but I have questioned myself. My sleep has been fitful at best. A few nights ago, I didn't sleep well because I was having nightmares all night. On my right shoulder was Benevolence, and she was saying, "You did the right thing; you knew what you were doing. You didn't do anything wrong; it was the right thing for everybody, including Woody". And then, on my left shoulder was the toxic monster Cruelty. Cruelty was yelling through my head to Benevolence, "You should've done this or that or didn't ask for help soon enough. You are a horrible person. You don't know what you're doing. Who are YOU that you can make decisions like this." I felt like a ping-pong ball all night listening to these arguments back and forth. The topography of feelings was wicked, and although I didn't wake up crying, it left me with a total sense of emptiness. Also, imposter syndrome. Sadness. Numbness. Exhaustion. Yes, that's the depression stage.

But during the next day, the feelings changed. I began to have more physical achiness (another sign of depression) and the distinct sensation of the weight of an elephant on my chest. My heart is fine physically, so no worries; it's just emotionally shattered. Most of you have been through loss. When doctors ask you to describe the type of pain you're feeling (usually physical, but it could be emotional, too), you might say grinding, burning, throbbing, shooting, achy, gnawing, etc... It brings up comments like "I feel like I was hit by a truck." These are the manifestations of our deep sense of loss. Our bodies become partners with our brains and hearts in moving the grief on.

The choice to turn to humane euthanasia is never easy or made casually. My shelter is one that will use it to provide peace and relieve suffering, so I am exposed to it more than most people. I have also counseled pet parents and cried with them as I guided them to that decision. The decision tree I must work through with my own animals is even more complicated. On one large branching trunk, I am trying to tease out Richard's and my emotions. Another branch questions what is best for our pet, and other branches carry the weight of what would be the outcome of not doing it. Is my pet actually suffering? What is their quality of life? Is extending their life for me or them? Can I handle the doubt (the battle of whether I made the right decision)? How will I balance my choice ethically and morally? Is it time?

Most people are very uncomfortable making such a weighty decision. I am not by any means comfortable, but I have a great deal of experience making it. I wish that was not true, but I am thankful I have that experience. It allows me to work through the branches of my tree, and I know I will reach the right decision, as morally confusing as it can be. It is on me, but especially with an animal I love and share my life with; it rips open my soul - every - single - time.

I am oscillating between periods of sadness, the desperate missing of his sweet soul, and suffocation by an elephant. Benevolence has won those early battles for now, so the doubts I had in those first few days are diminished for the time being. But it will take a long time to resolve the feelings and move through the mourning process. The important thing is that the feelings are in constant motion, and I think that's a good thing. I am watching Richard and myself to make sure we are both processing, which will lead to that acceptance and hope phase someday. Someday.

Faith may be grieving in her own way. Some of you may wonder if animals grieve. I believe they do. Observations of elephants, primates, whales, and other animals have shown they are aware of the death of family members and will stay near the body of the deceased for a time. Are they going through the same experience we do emotionally? The answer to this is unknown, but someday, we might know. I believe animals do not think about the past or future like we do. They live very much in the present. The future that dogs experience might be expectations related to routine (looking forward to food, a walk, or humans coming home), but I don't believe they do future planning (some of you with border collies may want to argue this point!). Their past is similar. Past events can predict current behavior, but they do not think and plan based on what has happened, at least not like we do.

I give animals a lot of credit for understanding their conspecifics much better than we think. Most of my dogs, I believe, have either had an awareness or have actually sensed physiological/electrical perceptions that indicated to them "something was off." I've had more than a few clients who reported that their dogs would incessantly paw at or lick an area of their human body. These clients later reported a personal medical problem- their own dogs were smelling something that wasn't right and were pointing to it. There are service dogs that sense and are trained to alert their people for blood sugar, seizures, and more. We even have psychiatric service dogs that alert for panic attacks, anxiety, and PTSD. How do they know? I think Faith knew something was wrong, so she easily accepted he was gone suddenly.

Because I so respect dogs' perceptions, I do not believe that my personal dogs need to be present to smell the body of their housemate to accept what happened. I think our dogs are so much more able to understand health and physical change than we can even imagine. They know long before we do. This is a highly personal decision, though. If this is something that makes you feel better and helps you, your family, and your animals, please carry on! No judgement here. You need to do what helps you!

For us, the sensation of him being gone is strange. We still "feel" his presence. Sometimes, we think we hear him banging around at night. We both long to touch him, feel his whiskers and lips, and look into those happy, sweet eyes. Some people would say yes, he is still there with us. I don't know that. We know he is gone from this physical plane. In time, I would like to think that he graced our lives for as long as we needed him, and someone, somewhere else, needed his pure, intense love more than we do. He has a new job. It's hard to just say we might not need him (how could we not need him?) because his love was intoxicating and addictive.

But we are strong and will make it. We are not selfish with either sharing him with the universe or about letting him go. I make no claims to understand the machinations of existence, and I admit that I make up stories not unlike my ancestors that help me get through the unexplainable parts of life. I hope he will keep an eye on us, just as we think about him.

Faith checked briefly for him in the backyard the first

night he was gone. She has been happy and peaceful since. We've been to the beach several times since he left, and Faith has joyfully galloped in large circles around us. She has been saying hi to dogs and people. Do I think she is mourning? No, for the most part. The only thing I have observed is she has been sleeping a lot. Is that because she is depressed or because he is not here bugging her to get up and play? Unknown. She most misses him at night when they would play after dinner. But she has started to solicit play from us at night, which we indulge. She will move quickly through this time. We can learn so much from our dogs.

So Woody's path has diverged from ours. We are sad it happened as we were looking forward to many happy years together on a singular road. He was an extraordinary dog. Safe travels, little man. Thank you for gracing and enriching our lives. We will always love you.

I believe that each person who listens to grief becomes a partner in sharing a minute part of it. If you have read this far, you have taken a teeny piece of my burden. Thank you. Don't hesitate to talk to me if you see me out and about. I'm happy to share.

If you are suffering from grief or depression and feel stuck, Please seek help. Call your doctor. Many professionals and protocols can assist you in feeling better soon.

It's a difficult read for me even now; I can't believe her brilliance in what she wrote.

I couldn't sleep, and when I collapsed at night, I had awful dreams and visions. I was seeing my doctors every week, but it wasn't helping. I was drinking more just to try to pass out for a couple of hours. The communication between my wife and I started to fall apart. I was writing my feelings and I think that's about the only thing that gave me a little peace.

On January 27th, I was driving home from a convention in Los Angeles. I had gotten together with my old friend Patrick. We had shared a hotel room for a couple of nights, and on the first night, we split a bottle of tequila - practice makes perfect. As I was driving home on Saturday afternoon, I got a call from my niece. For some reason, in one minute, she told me about her childhood, how her father had beaten her, and how my sister (her mom) had been complicit in the act. Suddenly, I remembered the abuse that I had taken from my parents…it left me gobsmacked and confused as to why Woody's loss was so devastating, and now the new awareness of this familial abuse as well.

During the next two weeks, I had a repetitive dream of my parent's grave. I have never been there, but I could see it clearly. I had never been told when either my mother or father had died until weeks later, but in my dream, I could see their graves. When I spoke with my therapist about it, and we investigated it, I told him that my parents had made me attend the funerals of people who were strangers to me, and they always made me look into the casket. I remembered that the only time we got together as a family was when somebody died. My therapist, in wisdom, said, "The reason you are having this dream is Woody died, and "they" are gathering. The realization struck me like a brick. I told them "to go home and leave me alone," and I never had the dream again.

January dissolved into early February. I had cracked a wisdom tooth and needed to have it removed. Because of my knee/total joint replacement, my surgeon required me to take a big dose of antibiotics before any dental work. I took my meds before surgery, which went well. The antibiotics upset my stomach horribly though, and somewhere around midnight on the night of surgery (Friday), I took a Percocet on an empty stomach. I threw up and was unable to eat until Sunday. On Monday morning, I lost a crown on the other side of my mouth. This meant a return trip to the dentist and more antibiotics.

I couldn't eat for about ten days after that visit. I lived on mashed potatoes and vodka. Slowly, I tried to add things like frozen peas to the mashed potatoes. I understood what starving was about, and my intestines were in constant upheaval. My stomach got worse. I was tired all the time as I was getting about two hours of sleep a night, and that was filled with

38

horrible dreams that I didn't understand. I found myself just standing and staring into space. I had no desire to do anything. Three or four drinks took care of some of the pain, but I was feeling worse all the time. I lost track of days. I had to write down when I had done the laundry and when I had shopped for food for Wendi. I was hopelessly lost. I didn't have an appetite. Food didn't look good to me, and when I tried to eat something normal, my intestines would revolt violently. I started dropping weight and was dehydrated. I felt miserable.

Chapter 7

March 2024

I still couldn't eat anything but the most bland things. I had moved on to chicken soup but was still keeping with the mashed potatoes. My mouth was beginning to feel better, but I still wasn't sleeping unless I had a lot of alcohol. I would break down. I know it was hard for Wendi to watch. There was nothing that I could do. Our communication was not good. My visits to the doctors resulted in me crying most of the time.

On March 13th, Wendi said I woke up screaming, "Woody's barking." I was still hearing him drink water in the backyard. I was trying to understand my grief, but it just wasn't going away. The nightmares were terrible, with the same dream every night. In my dream, I was standing in front of a huge open expanse; everything was gray, and there was no horizon. I'd wake up frustrated and disoriented.

I stopped journaling. When I tried to write out my feelings, I could sometimes understand them. But now that I had stopped writing altogether, my mind was just a jumble of thoughts about Woody.

I talked to my therapist, and we talked about how my feelings were real and that it was going to take some time for this to process. He mentioned being present for *messages and messengers,* and I tried to leave my grief long enough in case one showed up.

I couldn't work. I didn't feel like I had any kind of creative thoughts. I stopped playing music, something I had been able to lose myself in for over sixty years. I had no desire to pick up a guitar.

Chapter 8

April 2024

The first thing that I noticed in writing this book was that I didn't write in my journal at all for the month of April. I was finding myself sitting in a chair and just staring for long periods of time; then I'd start to cry. I was lost. I couldn't sleep. I was having the same dream every night of this big gray landscape without form. I still couldn't eat, but I was still drinking pretty heavily. I continued to reflect on my therapist's words of *messengers and messages,* but I still wasn't connecting that to my life.

Section 2 Healing

Chapter 9

May 2024 - The Road Back - The Dreams Start

My dreams had evolved into finding myself walking in that huge, gray, empty expanse, but Woody was walking with me. When I would wake up (this dream was so real to me), I couldn't stop crying for a long time.

On May 1st, a good friend allowed me to stay at his home on the bluff at Dillon Beach. It's about a four-hour drive up there, and when I got there, the wind off the water was blowing about thirty mph, and it was cold. I had stopped for food on the way, so I settled into the couch and just stared out the window. The ocean was beautiful, and I just sat there and stared until late in the evening, listening to the wind blow.

My sleep was fitful as the wind blew all night. I watched some shows on my iPad and kept staring out the window. I was a little afraid of going to sleep in a new place. I tried to imagine Woody was protecting me.

I awoke to a beautiful sunny day with no wind. I ate some toast and headed out for a walk on the beach. Music had been very important to me up to this point, and Sting's *Soul Cages* album was high on my list. The tide was low and I walked toward the end of the spit, about two miles long. I was listening to *Soul Cages* on my headphones, and I thought it would be really great to find a sand dollar. Enter Miracle #1

I looked down to my feet, and a perfect sand dollar appeared. I was a little surprised to find it. I felt it was a gift from Woody.

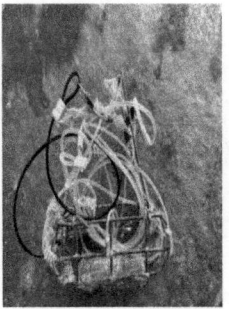

I walked on and looked ahead, and Miracle #2 appeared. A bait cage was tangled in the seaweed, a soul cage. This find really took me back.

I spent the rest of the ninety-minute walk marveling at the gifts that I had just been given. They didn't relieve my grief, but they were a sign that there was a bigger power out there. There was no wind.

I love the countryside in that area and find a lot of peace in driving Highway 1 down to Pt. Reyes Station. I found a restaurant and had what I considered my first meal since late January: a hamburger and fries. My stomach rumbled and complained, but I got through it.

I drove back to Dillion Beach as the wind was picking up. Once again, I found myself on the couch with a guitar in my hands, staring out the window until way past dark. My dreams started to show some forms in the gray horizon, but I couldn't make out anything distinctly.

I woke the next morning with no wind, and heading down

to the beach again, I took a different path. I was simply amazed at how beautiful the scene was (this photo was to become my screen saver).

I sat on the beach and decided as the wind picked up that I would drive home along the coast. I thought as I drove that I was filling my mind with the beauty that was the coast of California…what a gift.

When I got home I was standing with Faith and Wendi in the backyard when I noticed a beautiful moth that was on the wall above the window directly under where I slept. Messages and messengers went through my head and I knew it was Woody in the form of that moth welcoming me home. I stared at it for the longest time and told it good night and thank you. That night I had a crazy dream that I was flying around the backyard. In the morning, the moth was gone.

May 21

My therapist and I talked in my session that day about bringing the joy that Woody had brought me into my heart and to hold onto joy with the multi-armed bond of an octopus. We also discussed my new safe place at Dillon Beach.

My dream had changed into seeing Woody far out on the horizon. I was in my safe place, but it was frustrating to me that I couldn't reach him. It was like he was playing with me. It was like he was playing with me. I had the same dream for about three days until I realized there was a joy he was showing in avoiding me (I'm reminded of him running crazy on by the school) and that I could bring that joy into my heart. I thought of a moment at Dillon Beach when a bird had landed on the railing outside the window. I had thought it was you (Woody) and that you were there to protect me.

On the 28th, my dreams changed from the gray horizon I had seen so many times into a vast expanse of drawers that I couldn't open. I also had my regular dream of Woody on the horizon and I couldn't get to him.

May 30th

At therapy, we worked on playing with Woody on the horizon, that I should invite him to play with me, and that I should play with him. I understood it as transference that

Woody was part of a different dimension that was just as real as the ones we inhabit if I could only tune into that frequency. This gave me a sense of awe and wonder, what a privilege to be a part of it.

June 3rd

I don't do anniversaries well, and this was the 5th month since we lost Woody. At 5 am, Faith woke up in the front room and shook, and it woke me up. I got up and went into the bathroom and there was a brilliant bright light coming through the window. My neighbor can be an early bird but this wasn't her car lights or porch light. I slid open the window for a better look. About six feet outside the window there was an intensely bright sphere of light that was hovering. I was amazed at what I was seeing, but it was very real. I stood in the bathtub and just watched it. After what seemed like a couple of minutes, it moved out of my sight into the front yard. We keep a pile of shells near our entry path; when I went outside later, they were scattered about, nothing broken, just scattered all over.

My therapist recommended a dream healer in the North Bay. I contacted Ophilia Mandara and set up an appointment for early July. I kept having the same dream every night of Woody on the horizon and this expanse of nothing, except now it had become dimensional and was slanting at about twenty degrees.

One of the requirements for working with Ophilia was to describe my intent. I took a deep dive into my emotions to express my intention. During this time, I wrote the following in my journal: "I believe any life-altering event brings you to a crossroads, and if you truly want to heal, you have to embrace that event fully. I believe with the proper intent of not only relieving your personal pain, this experience can also help others, but it must be done without ego. You must take a journey into the depths of your soul, and in the bottom, no matter how dark, there is joy and the root of all feelings".

6-18 From my Journal

I woke up last night and felt a wind blow across my face; I thought it was Woody. Later, when I was weeding in the backyard, a beautiful dove landed beside me, messengers and messages. [WN1]

6-21 From my Journal

Somedays, I just sit and stare. I realize how much of my time you demanded and how it frustrated me at times; other times, I loved it.

Section 3

In my Dreams

Up to this point, I've written in the first person as much as possible; when I started my work with Ophilia, things began to change rapidly. I am going to include the notes from the thirteen sessions I had with her.

As I prepared for my first session with Ophilia, my dreams shifted. She had asked me, "How does your intention feel in your body." The following are my dreams in the first person.

6-28

In my dreams I was standing in a gray room with a 45-degree slant to the walls, then Woody walked in from the right side.

6-29

The next night, I am observing a flat, gray room, and I can see a black stick made out of wenge wood that someone gave me a piece of wood that was in the garage.

6-30

I am standing on a slanted floor; the room appears

seamless, but I can balance on the slant. Off to my right, I see something sticking out of the wall. I walk up to it (still on the slanted floor) and hear a voice, "It's wood."

7-1

I am standing on a slanted floor again; off to my right are square pegs that poke through a white wall.

Shortly after Woody passed, when I was standing in the bathroom, looking in the mirror, I remembered right after his death I would look in the mirror and think that I was disappearing. When I was in the bathroom this morning, I saw the same thing today, and I reflected on the grief that I felt. I was sure it would crush me it was so intense.

7-3

I am standing in the same room, and for the first time, I can see to the left. I was looking to my right, and I could turn my head to the left. When I looked in that direction, I could see a big gray box or table. I just stared at it.

Section 4
Ophilia Mandara - Dreams Come Alive

I'm not sure how to tell this part of the story. Starting on July 3rd, 2024, I started thirteen weeks of intensive dream research with Ophilia. During our first meeting in mid-June, she had tasked me to come up with a single sentence of my intent for the work we were about to do. I spent many hours on what I wanted to say; in the end, this is what I came up with and shared with her. "It is my intent to grow through this grief into a more peaceful and powerful life."

The sessions were conducted over Zoom, and I seemed to experience an altered state where we would explore my dreams. Ophilia led me to the depths of my dreams, and somehow, I came out on the other side.

During our first session, I came to realize that while I was dreaming, I was out of body. If I had been in body, I would be dreaming of being in bed, so I had to accept the fact that there was a *Dream Richard* that could travel during my dreams.

During our session, she would ask me to find three anchor points that I could reflect on over the coming week. It was my "job" to take the three anchor points and try to form them into the composite of one anchor point. It took me several weeks to be able to form a composite. Here we go.

Dreamwork Session #1 July 3rd

The first dream we worked on was the one in which I was standing in a gray plane with slanted floors. During the session, Ophilia guided me through the dream. Here are the three anchor points that *Dream Richard* encountered.

These are Ophilia's words.

1. In Dream Richard, in response to the green color and the awareness "that's where Woody lives" -- warmth, a sensation of love, and never wanting it to end, pressed into the head, neck, arms, and chest, as though holding him. A definite odor - the way he smells.

2. In Dream Richard, feeling the balance despite the slanted floor. A lightness in the legs that moves upward into the spine, "like I could do a backflip" - a subtle sense of insecurity, starting in the thighs, moving up into the spine, feeling the muscles as though about to move into a flip

3. In the shimmering heat wave seen on the slanted floor, a sense of belly dancing in the orange-red shimmer, a sense of deep exhaustion in the movement and feeling.

Here are the reflections I wrote later that afternoon.

Gratitude isn't a feeling that I have had since losing Woody; although I know that it's out there, it just seems to elude me.

July 6th

Last night, while dreaming my #3 anchor point, the shimmering heat wave turned into an orange ball, perfectly centered in my dream's field of view.

July 7th

In my dream, I am standing in a big field in front of a large building that is reflecting light. In my second dream of the night, our backyard is like a skating rink, and Faith is sliding across like a slip-and-slide, really enjoying herself.

July 8th

I've felt like writing a poem, but I can't hold onto any thoughts. I keep hoping that this feeling wears off, that I can bring it to the surface and not bury my feelings so deeply. I feel like I am pushing through the surface, pushing through the skin.

Dreamwork Session #2 July 10th

These were the three anchors from our session that Ophilia chose for the composite that I was to work on during the week:

1. In Dream Richard, standing in the water - an expressway, a tube between the feet and heart, "feels good," moves very fast

2. In Dream Faith, gliding, moving without expending energy, a sense of fun in the spine, tail, ears -- tail keeping balance

3. In Dream Richard seeing Dream Woody watching Dream Faith feels hard, a black, smooth, empty feeling in the heart

These were Ophilia's observations.

"I wanted to reflect that the first and third anchor points for this composite are very relevant to one another. This session offered some potent heart medicine. This is where we get into the alchemy of holding distinct feelings simultaneously -- now the "expressway" gets to assist the more challenging feelings that arise in the heart. The earth is involved too - the feet opening up the heart."

July 15th

I hadn't remembered my dreams for a few nights, so I didn't write anything. Making notes, even in the middle of the night, seemed to help me better understand my pain, my dreams, and my healing, although I couldn't see the healing yet.

I woke up at 4 am, and I tried to work with my anchors from our session on the 10th of July. As I was meditating on them, out of somewhere between my 1st and 2nd anchor, a black spot appeared in my lower left vision. In my meditation, I was viewing the black spot, and as I concentrated on it, the spot turned into a black fog.

Ophilia and I had discussed what blackness meant in dreams, and she made the observation that the *blackest soil was the most fertile*, where the best things grew; she had encouraged me to approach the blackness in my dreams and not be afraid of them. This was and is an enormous realization for me to this day. She also discussed welcoming my dream life before I went to sleep. This has become very evolved since then, and I practice this welcoming to this day as well.

July 18th

Before I went to sleep, I welcomed my dream life into my sleep. At about 4 am, I was awakened by a dream in which I was standing in the gray-slanted plane, where I was standing in front of a huge box full of mashed potatoes and frozen peas. The dream didn't strike me as strange at all as what I had been able to eat: mashed potatoes with frozen peas mixed in. My digestion issues remained; I was still drinking fairly heavily, between two to three strong vodka and cranberry drinks a night.

Also, around this time, I was walking close to two miles a day barefoot at the beach. While I was there, I was focused on a meditation of sorts around the anchor points in my dreams. At this time, I began wearing earbuds and listening to a very few select albums, Sting's *Soul Cages* and Dave Matthews Band *Under the Table and Dreaming*, both of which became  the background for my meditation and walks. At this time, I was being given amazing gifts from the ocean. This is a whale tooth, and it's a pretty rare find.

Dreamwork session #3 July 20th

I only had two anchor points to build my composite on this week; they are below with Ophilia's observations.

1. Vastness before you, arms open and feet in the sand, "ready to receive," a sense of loss and anticipation

2. In the brown, orange, pink seaweed, "interconnected" -- Rooted and swaying. "Pulse of the water" strongly felt in the back, and also "it's all me."

This is Ophilia's response:

It occurs to me to offer the reminder that as you work with the composite, you can also continue to work with the spoken or word-based intention before sleeping. This can be done separately rather than trying to weave it directly into the composite. It could be like an opening prayer before you sit with the composite or as a closing prayer. This could be as simple as speaking your overall intention aloud before or after working the composite. You may already be weaving this in your own fashion, but I offer it up as I think it will help to keep our compass aimed at your personal north star, so to speak :)

After this session, it became clear that I would have a deeper understanding as I said aloud my intentions and help in working with the composite. During this session, Black equals Growth became very apparent.

59

I don't remember any of my dreams from that week, at least I didn't write them down but I had a very interesting experience in working with the composite. We had purchased a new van and I flew to San Diego to pick it up and drive it home. It was an early flight and we were at cruising altitude as the sun came up over the left wing. With the clouds, it was truly beautiful. I asked myself if I thought it would be wonderful to sit on the nose of the plane and get a 360 degree of the scene. I closed my eyes, began meditating on the idea, and low and behold, Dream Richard was out there, sitting on the nose of the plane, feeling the cold wind and experiencing the beauty of the sunrise. I didn't stay long, maybe two minutes, but it was a very real and profound experience.

July 29th Dream

Dream Richard is overlooking a field with a black obelisk to my left. I feel it's over five feet tall and about two feet square. Objects are moving from my left to my right, and clearly, I hear "On The Line."

July 31st Dream

As I walked and before sleep, I began vocalizing my gratitude and asking for wisdom from my dreams. It was a very tough day; I had overwhelming grief for Woody, and I cried through my shower and most of the day.

August 1st

Today, when I was walking at the beach, I found some seaweed that was bright green and pink, some of the colors that I had begun to experience with Dream Richard. I stood on the seaweed in the water and just felt how much colder it felt than the surrounding water and kelp. I meditated on my anchor points as I stood there.

Dreamwork #4 Aug. 3rd

These were my anchor points for my composite from Dreamwork session #4. I chose to allow her to help me with the anchor points as I'm very involved with what's happening in the dream.

From Ophilia.

It is wonderful to hear that the session has been a profound one for you, and I look forward to hearing more about how it supports you and works with you over the next week.

1. In Dream, Richard walking on the plane, a sense of sinking under the feet, a little cool, like quicksand, a sense of "humbled, "wonder" that rises through the whole body like smoke

2. In Dream, Richard in response to the silver fish-like lights, "I want to welcome them in" a sense of welcoming in the chest and hands, "a gift that is equally important"

3. In the obelisk, a fear of the unknown below, slippery, constriction in the heart

After the session, I spent a long time meditating on what had just happened. I felt in my feet the sensation of slowly sinking into the earth. I felt the smoke from the sage I was burning rise up into my heart. I felt the feeling of humble wonder of being able to hold the light sensation of knowing that the sensation was Woody, and now that sensation of humble wonder is his special gift to me.

August 3rd Dream

Dream Richard walked into a vast and endless visual plane. As I stared, I could see endless tents set up in perfectly straight and arranged rows.

August 4th Dream

I entered the vast plane from the left. To my right, I saw a figure like a Japanese Samurai. There was a movement toward me, and some fear on my part. The big black box was to my left in my vision.

August 6th Dream

Dream Richard is standing on the slanted vast plane, but the road or path that was straight before has now become very curvy.

August 7th Dream

Dream Richard enters the same plane or room as the previous night. The road is still curved, but instead of being all gray, I am now seeing a lot of the colors green and red.

Dreamwork Session #5 Aug. 8th

Again, I chose to allow Ophilia to define the anchor points for the composite.

From Ophilia:

Here are the notes on the anchors from today's session.

1. In Dream, Richard standing on the bluff, an immense sense of wonder in the heart and in front of the body, a sense that "I can look at anything and I can be conscious that this it's there" - "I am so lucky."

2. In Dream, Richard standing in the river, a sense of the river moving by the feet, connected and rootedness to the earth

3. In the motion of the river, gratitude moving between the feet and the heart, "What a gift" -- "I'm grateful that he visits me."

I'm also including a note of what you spoke aloud while holding the composite together: a sense that "there is so much to learn, and it humbles me" "I am so grateful."

August 11th Dream

Last night, I realized there are now two rooms in my dream, when I am in room one, I am working on "other" things. I don't know what those other things are. Room 2 is where I go to work on me; again, I'm not sure what this means, but there are now two distinct rooms in my dreams.

Dreamwork Session #6 Aug. 15th

From Ophilia:

Beautiful work today. It seems we touched on some very important "ingredients" for this tincture.

Here are the anchors:

1. In Dream Richard, standing above the "silos/rooms" -- arms outstretched, energy coming into the palms and up the arms - pumping like blood - happiness - a green color. All connecting in the heart.

2. In the thin, white, almost transparent fabric, meandering in the air, a sieve or strainer - a filter in the heart. Grief that comes through and goes back. "It's not one way."

August 15th

After the session from my journal

I felt completely depleted. I was confident that I had made huge strides in my grief before session six and that I was moving forward. Now, I feel that I have to rebuild from scratch. I need to keep intent and focus with wonder and humility.

August 16th Dream

When I woke up as Dream Richard, I was looking at two

black circles in my field of vision; they were very predominant taking over almost my entire view of the gray landscape.

August 17th Dream

Last night, as I was observing the black circles in my dream, they exploded in front of me into a mass of green and black. The explosion was violent and shook me so jarringly that I felt in my very soul.

Later that morning, when I took a walk, a crab grabbed a hold of my toe and wouldn't let it go, *messages and messengers*, I wondered if it was Woody, and it made me cry and yet happy at the same time.

August 19th

While I was in the backyard, I found a bunch of Woody's hair that came out of a grooming brush. The find took me off my feet, and I was overcome with grief. I cried really hard for fifteen minutes. When Wendi saw me, she told me she thought I might be depressed, and that made me feel really bad. I could see how much stress she was under dealing with me, and her label of depression was her reaction to me being completely broken down.

These intense grief and crying sessions would sometimes come over me in the shower, and I'd just weep for ten minutes and let the hot water comfort me.

Dreamwork Session #7 Aug. 22nd

From Ophilia

Here are the anchor points for this week's 'tincture.'

1. In Dream Richard on the cliffside path, standing straight up, a sense of amazement: I can stand tall, see the beauty, and not be afraid to fall. A sense of strength in the legs and heart.

2. In Dream Richard first seeing the blue towel, shock and awe, a sense of push and pull, being drawn in, and also feeling afraid.

3. In the robin egg blue towel, between the sand, stone, and ground and the bones, a sense of doing a job, protective, supportive, keeping the sand off.

"Beautiful work today -- it is immense work, and you are right where the work is calling you to be. Thank you for your presence, courage, and depth."

This session really threw me off. I was so shaken when I saw the bones on the blue towel, especially when I realized they were Woody's bones mixed with my bones. I was in shock. When Ophilia directed me not to be shocked by the bones emotionally but to experience how it felt in my body, it was like an electric shock.

We ordered blue bath towels for the bathroom so I could apply Ophilia's anchor point of the blue towel in my dream of being protective and supportive. I was reaching out for anything that would help me feel better.

August 25th Dream

In my dream that night, Dream Richard was in a room that appeared to have many exits, but I had no direction as to which one to take. I could hear a lot of noise, but I couldn't identify where it was coming from or even what type of sound it was. Dream Richard stayed in the room for a long time, just looking around and listening.

Dreamwork Session #8 Aug. 29th

Ophilia's notes from this session.

Here is the tincture from today's session:

1. In Dream, Richard standing in the room with many exits, the right foot lower than the left, a continuous sense of light, holding you in the solar plexus, keeping you balanced - "I can just be there" "not conscious of trying"

2/3. A sense of softness, comfort, strength, and "light circulation of air" in the left side, covered like a coat... and in the right side, a sense of just hanging out in space, as though the ground has dropped away

Thank you for your potent work today. It strikes me that in both anchors, there is a contrast in the right/left sides: one foot lower than the other, and a clear contrast between right and left in the second anchor. Some potent re/balancing at play...

When she said some potent rebalancing was underway how correct she was. Although I was still being overcome by grief and crying a lot, which I'm sure was hard on Wendi. I was beginning to be able to accept that I could understand that Woody was still with me, and that created continuity in my life. I was still dreaming vividly at night and instead of waking up disturbed, I was waking with a feeling of understanding of my feelings, a huge shift.

August 30th Dream

As Dream Richard observed the twisty road in front of me, the road suddenly went straight. I sat down beside of the road. I felt that there was a blue force covering my left shoulder. I sat a long time under that protection.

September 3rd Dream

Dream Richard is sitting on the left side of the road, watching the road over my left shoulder. As I was watching the road, Woody appeared out of the background; he was the size of a Macy's Thanksgiving day balloon.

Dreamwork Session #9 Sept. 5th

Ophilia's notes from session 9: It's the beginning for me of taking all the composites and anchors and letting Dream Richard work them into my real life. This was a huge session for me; it stayed with me for days. Look at Ophilia's words below. I still read them over and over.

Here are the notes from today's session:

1. In the solar plexus, legs, feet, and butt, a vibrational energy/pulse - "your heartbeat" and a sense of connection -- feeling these two roads are a part of you. (Noting here that you felt an awareness that the road you are connected to in your lower body is one that 'you won't walk again' and that the left path is where the journey lies. You are still connected to the path in your low body - it is what got you here.)

2. In the transition from gray to blue in the sky, a flow that starts in the heart, flows up over the head, and expands into the gray/blue, like a tulip -- "awe."

3. In filling Balloon Woody with all the love, feeling lighter, still connected, but lighter, in the heart and shoulders.

If you're comfortable with it and it feels authentic to you, I want to offer you an exercise this week, which is to add a little bit to your intention and dream incubation process. The invitation would be about asking the 'allies in the darkness' to

72

present themselves in an accessible way (of course, framing this in whatever way works for you.) This is by no means mandatory, but since it came up today, I wanted to offer it to you as an option of adapting your intention-setting process to focus in on that aspect of the work.

I also wanted to add that the whole process of befriending darkness can be very multi-layered and is sometimes not what we expect. What I've often seen is that we may experience a lot of challenge, sorrow, and "darkness" in our daily lives, but when we look under the hood, so to speak, as we do in dream work, we may be met with very expansive realities of wonder, awe and gratitude. Conversely, we may experience a lot of joy and levity in our daily lives; but when we look at the inner landscape, some more challenging emotions may present themselves. I believe that these energies, all of them - those that are challenging and those that are expansive, want to live, and will always be present. Where and how they show up will, of course, be different for each person. What we do not exercise regularly (what we do not make apparent and get intimate with) will likely creep up on us or even disrupt us from more unconscious places. Sometimes, I think our challenging periods are exactly this - the exercising of sorrow or pain so that we can make these states more conscious and live them out until it is time for a new, energetic chapter. I leave this here as food for thought rather than didactic truth :)

As is my preferred approach. These areas have so many labyrinthian ways of moving and expressing, but this is part of what I found myself thinking about during our session and conversation.

As always, it is such an honor to work with you. I'll see you next week.

During this period, I was feeling very dark, that I was engulfed in it and the dark fog wouldn't lift. I worked with my anchors and spent time meditating at night before sleep but I could not lift the oppressive feeling. The above session started to shed some light on how I was feeling; it was quite comforting.

Dreamwork Session #10 Sept. 12th

Ophilia's notes and my anchor points from this session. I remember I cried through most of it, mostly from the loss of Woody, but also, there were tears of joy as I was realizing that I was changing and help was there for me to access.

Richard,

What a potent session today! I myself am humbled by the way you are navigating such profound waves. Thank you for the reminder of our immense and magical nature!

Here are the notes I have from today's session. They are a bit unorthodox compared to the usual "anchor" notes because I have included some notes that felt less like "anchors" per se but important expressions.

1. Pushing against the dinosaur egg - pressure in the hands moving upward and all the way down the arms into the core. Fear of pushing too hard but meeting no resistance.

2. In the Green Moving Minnow-like presences, motion, liquid through the entire body, expansive, "I'm a part of it," "Fortunate to be a part of it."

3. In the gratitude for being brought here by Woody: "I couldn't have gotten here without him," "the pain and darkness have all been necessary to humble me before myself

4. A continuation of the last point, "On my knees in front of the altar of the world. Joy and magic.

I will note that at the end, you joined this last anchor point to the position of being on the road, with the road and world before you.

I was very disoriented after this session. When I feel that way, I do something that requires no thought process on my part, so what I did was clean my backyard. As I was operating the blower, I looked down and saw this egg; there was no reason for it to be there. It was too late in the year for nests. I set it aside and went on with my chores. The egg stayed on Wendi's planting table for about three days. We had big winds and some rain, but the egg remained on the table until I realized that it was a very special gift that was directly related to my last session with Ophilia. It was quite a miracle.

9-15 From My Journal

Today, as I was walking on the beach, I found myself completely alone at the apex of my walk. When I started my walk back, I stopped and addressed the ocean. When I prayed I was able to humble myself in front of myself. I wept at the water's edge for quite a while. On reflection, I realized what had happened to me was something my therapist and I had talked about lately, about being able to view the world without my ego getting in the way.

Dreamwork Session #11 Sept. 19th

Ophilia's notes

Thank you for such a potent last session. I so enjoy our conversation and explorations of the "realer than real"!

Here are the anchors from today:

1. Sitting cross-legged in this bright space, with the road going off to the left. Foggy behind, clear ahead, taking it all in. "So Wonderful" "Allowing awareness to be elevated, because it is all good." Starts in the core and moves up to the shoulder, "tells me to relax."

2. In the "big foot walk," one foot after the other, "so aware" sensation in the feet, legs, and breath on the left ear. "Continuity" -- not sorrow, not determination, continuity.

During this session, towards the end, the breath that I felt on my left ear was that of Woody's. It shocked me at first, but then I began to understand continuity.

Sept 19th From my journal

During my walk, my prayers changed. I was now able to thank and bow to all of my companions and allies, both known and unknown. I was also able to bow to myself and honor myself in the work that I was doing.

Dreamwork session #12 Sept. 26th Wrap-up

I wasn't sure that I was ready for the sessions to end. Usually, they were only nine sessions long, but I had extended my time and our work together. I was afraid that I wasn't strong enough to go on without Ophilia's guidance. I found out during our wrap-up that I was wrong.

Ophilia's notes:

Richard,

Thank you so much for your presence this morning. I can't say enough what an honor it has been working with you and your potent team of allies. Here are the notes and the recording from today.

Words on the new path:

Thoughtful, Aware, Present, Honor

Additionally, "continuity" -- the path that someone built before you, not being alone on the road.

An invitation: What sensations in the body come with these words and awarenesses?

Words on the PTSD space that can be gently considered with those from above:

Panic, Isolation. Cold all day.

The intention as it is now:

"Keep my focus on living a more full and loving life. Understanding that this also means respect for myself."

Some suggested practices moving forward:

Continuing to tend the altar of items that has grown over the last few months. Finding a place among them for your words. Use this place as a space for prayer and declaration: sharing your gratitude for what this team and collective of allies has offered you, as well as a place to ask for support with your intention - as it evolves!

And from our brief anchor/embodiment practice:

A sense of gratitude for all the allies. Gratitude in the heart, hands, feet, arms. A sense that you can reach out and let them in. That although they are unseen - they aren't!

The long blue bus, full of your allies. A place you can walk up and down the aisles and check-in.

They are always there in the corral and along for the ride.

In Between - Redemption Begins

My sessions with Ophilia ended on September 26th. I'm going to let you read my response to her after I had two days to land back on the ground. The blue bus we had found with Dream Richard stayed in my thoughts. I wrote to her on the 28th of September, and the email from me was titled:

Evolutionary Intention call - the gift that keeps giving.

I've established a sacred area for myself with all of the allies gathered around me. I went for a walk at the ocean this morning, and it had totally changed for me. Before, I felt like it was my holy place; I don't feel that welcoming spirit now, but I do feel it in the space I created. I've instilled the words, and I feel great direction from seeing them. And I know that it will evolve.

Get on the blue bus, Gus....so I'm able to walk up and down the aisles and feel or see my allies on the seats; some are light, some are a little scary, some are just feeling or presence. But they are all on my blue bus, and we're on this ride together.

Let my intentions be the driving force for my new life............again, my eternal gratitude.

These are my reflections on my email:

"The title of this email is so very true. I can't begin to thank

81

you, Ophilia, for accepting me and being on this journey with me., so here we go.....so many things have changed for me since Thursday. I was completely taken off my feet after we finished; I felt lost. I've spent the last 48 hours thinking about where we have been in the past 12 weeks, an incredible journey, not for the faint of heart. It takes courage.

Magic

I stopped writing in my journal at this time and tried to understand my new way of living. Then something completely magical and unexpected happened to me - I stopped drinking alcohol on September 27th at 3:15 in the afternoon.

I have been a very experienced drinker (two to four drinks a day) for fifty-three years. Alcohol was my first choice for pain relief of any kind because it acted so quickly in my system. At 3 pm every day, a bell would start to ring in my head, demanding a drink; the more I delayed, the louder it got. Sometimes, I drank to the point of being drunk. I had used alcohol heavily after Woody died, and then I would become super emotional. I know that was hard for Wendi to see. Communication between us started to get very rocky. Wendi's mother had been a severe alcoholic, and I'm sure there was PTSD involved in her response as she watched me sink deeper into depression over Woody.

When I stopped, I was sitting in my music room with a guitar in my lap and a drink on the console. I looked down at the drink and said to myself, "I don't need or want this anymore. If I am going to walk a deeper path of intention, alcohol can't be a part of it because it could redirect my mind." That was it. Done with booze after fifty-three years.

My body revolted. I had horrible headaches, intense

intestinal distress, and sleeplessness like I had never experienced before. My body craved alcohol, but my brain didn't. I was down for a week with the initial withdrawal symptoms. I spoke with my doctor but didn't tell him I quit until the second or third conversation. He was encouraging but told me that this reaction was going to last for a few weeks and that I just kind of needed to tough it out until the alcohol worked its way out of my body and my brain. It was a tough couple of weeks.

As I write this today, I am still alcohol-free. I don't feel a desire for a drink, even when I'm around people drinking. My body is returning to a normal state. My dental hygienist could not believe how much better my gums looked. My persistent morning chest and nasal congestion cleared up in a week. My gut returned to what I think is normal (considering it had been all those years of abuse), and I was better able to control my emotions. I was still experiencing waves of complete grief, but I was able to call upon my allies and control my reaction to the waves.

Wendi and I started communicating much better. She saw how hard the first few weeks were on me physically, and she was there with comfort and support. My doctor was thrilled, although he was slightly confused at how it had happened to me but thrilled. My therapist was not surprised and was very supportive.

While I was going through the worst couple of days of quitting, I got an email from Ophilia.

Greetings Richard!

Thank you so much for your message. Indeed, this work is not for the faint of heart - and you've shown up impeccably for it all. I appreciate your willingness to be with the full spectrum. It can be ineffably challenging and is often so worth the energy it takes - expanding presence and recognition of life's mysterious teachings, beauty, and tenderness.

It sounds like you've welcomed the sacred and holy deeper into your home. Where you once felt it in this wild place, it is now closer at hand. And yes - it will continue to evolve!

I'm sending deep praise, recognition, and appreciation to you and your team, the bus, and beyond!

Thank you for this update, and please do continue to stay in touch should any other notes arise.

I am thinking of that Octavia Butler quote. All that we touch we change; all that we change changes us. I'm paraphrasing, but I think you will follow :) Thank you for participating in this path of change. It takes courage!

Yes, it takes courage.

Rebirth

Things were happening to me that I hadn't felt in close to a year. I found that I could work again, that I wanted to work again. I felt creative when I was editing a video. I had ideas like I used to have, and I could lose myself in the work. When I'm editing a music video or a documentary, I can be deeply involved in what I am doing, losing track of time altogether. After Woody's loss, I didn't sit in front of the computer until October. I did do enough to keep things going, but it was a chore, and I found no joy in it. I also found I could become deeply involved in music again. I was playing for about an hour a day and even starting to write music. I could feel things changing.

On October 6th, I emailed Ophilia to give her the update after she shared some of her new music with me. This is what I sent her:

Thank you for sharing that beautiful music this morning, really brightened my morning after a rough night staying on the bus with my allies.

Here's the craziest thing. Since our last session, I haven't had or felt the desire for alcohol. It's been with me for over fifty years, and since losing Woody, I have been hitting it pretty hard. At 3 pm, it's like a bell goes off in my head, and I have two drinks, maybe three a day. It is really amazing and such an expression of outward change to mirror what is going on inside. I never expected it. As I was sitting in front of my altar, I got a distinct message that if I wanted to walk and work with my allies, alcohol wasn't in the picture. I listened.

It's been quite a shock to my physical body. I'm just beginning to feel normal. I'm in touch with my GP, and he's thrilled. The journey continues, but somebody already built the road.

This was her response.

What a deep treasure it was to read this email. Please forgive my slow email cadence! And know your words have been with me all week.

This update is so potent. I am overjoyed to hear that the channel of communication with your allies has been clear and available.

I can't help but think about how, in many spiritual traditions and practices, there is often a "sacrifice" necessary in times of initiation. By this, I do not mean sacrificing a life - but instead, it is common that behaviors, habits, or lifestyle choices are called up to be released when the path deepens. I am holding this moment for you with great tenderness and care - as well as celebration and reverence for the personal path of initiation that you are walking.

I am glad, too, to hear that your GP is available as a

resource as you care for your body in this palpable shift. I am feeling the allies around you - seen and unseen!

Thank you for listening to my song. I trust it came in the right timing and am grateful for your listening ears. My prayer is that these creations are medicine to those who receive!

During this time, I was reading "When Things Fall Apart - Heart Advice for Difficult Times" by Pema Chodron. The book had a very strong effect on me. At times, I had to read a section three or four times during the week before I could understand how to apply it to my life, emotions, and the changes that I was experiencing.

October 12th Dream and Result

On the 12th I started to have a repetitive dream which I had for the next three nights. The dream would come about 4 am every night. I had a huge meeting for a possible documentary project the following Tuesday. For three nights before that meeting, I had this repeating dream that I was on the outside of a circle at night. I could see light and beings but I couldn't identify any of the shapes as human or energy.

On Tuesday, at the ninety-minute meeting, I completely opened my heart to someone who appeared to accept it. He was very enthusiastic about my participation, and I thought we were kindred spirits. I spent Tuesday night sending over notes and again Wednesday morning, and then all went silent. It was very upsetting to me. I felt I had done everything correctly and didn't understand their silence. I thought I had failed.

I spent Thursday at 4 am out under the moon in my backyard, barefoot, my feet in the dirt, and prayed aloud for guidance and direction, and then I remembered the dream of being outside of the circle. By 6 am, I felt completely healed and whole by realizing it was nothing I did. It just wasn't meant to be.

I took a walk at the ocean as the full moon set Friday morning and felt full. I've enclosed a picture from that walk, the line from Sting playing in my head, *"and I swam with the moon and her lover, till I lost sight of the land"* ...potent stuff.

It takes courage.

October 29thDiary

I realized that I hadn't written in my journal for quite a while, and I needed to start again. I had been writing emails so I had a record of how fast things were moving for me and what I was experiencing. Writing my way through what I am thinking or experiencing is a way to establish clarity in what I'm feeling. I've been journaling for almost forty years and I find it as useful today as I did when I started.

From my journal:

I thought I had reached the bottom of my grief. What I'm learning is that there is no bottom, only darkness. As I thought about it, I realized that I needed to make friends with the blackness of my grief. I realized without a bottom, there is no way to the top of the hill. I watched the moon as it disappeared, and I felt like I was disappearing as well, and that wasn't a bad thing; in fact, the old me, the person who held onto grief, was disappearing, and I was beginning to heal, that may be in making friends with the worst of the feelings, I've started on the way back to the top.

November 1st

I met with my therapist and discussed some of my dreams. We had talked about ceremony some in the past but I felt like I needed to understand more.

One of his recommendations going forward was to dig a hole in my backyard and stand in it for grounding. I had stumbled on it by accident. I continue this practice to this day and find much comfort and relief in it.

November 3rd Journal

When you face what you think is the very bottom, make friends and send the blackness love, or it will become a stone in your pathway.

November 3-4 Dreams

From an email from me to Ophilia:

I've had a couple of interesting repetitive dreams, and I've decided to enlist Dream Richard as an Ally rather than somebody I don't understand.

In 1st dream...we have a small, narrow skylight in our hallway; Dream, Richard is inside that skylight looking down, and Woody is walking back and forth in the hall below. When I woke up, I felt as if I really had been up in the skylight looking down.

2nd dream was a follow-up to sitting beside my slanting road, and next to me were two compression suits. There was no form to them; as I sat there, from behind came my parents. I could feel every time my father hit me, his belt; my mom used a rake and a switch. The pain was very real, and I felt it went on for twenty minutes.

When I woke up, I was out of my body. What I think I was feeling was a rebirth; that was the compression suit. When Wendi left for work, I got out by myself and cleared my mind and heart; then, I invited all the pain and darkness that I felt into my heart and sent it out as love. I was OK in a couple of hours where it would have taken days before.

November 10

I was in contact with Ophilia. She had remembered from our sessions that I was a Capricorn. I barely know enough about astrology to understand a fortune cookie, but she shared this with me on November 10. I had no idea what was going to be revealed to me on the 19th of November, the day Pluto left its current cycle.

Ophilia sent me this email:

"I share this with you, for one, because it was sort of knocking on the door of my psyche and wanting to be shared, and for two, because of what you've shared about the abuse from your parents, the pain, and the idea of sharing your story. First, I want to say that I'm sending so much love and care to that earlier version of yourself that went through such heartbreaking and awful treatment. Additionally, I will share that these are exactly the types of situations that Pluto points to — the misuse of power and tragic abuses from parents or authority figures. The Real hauntings that we can experience in this world. Oftentimes, transits from Pluto urge us to confront these aspects of life and stand in the strength of our stories. To find those seeds in ourselves that can be liberated from the shackles of the past, fully empowered in the now - while still fully honoring and giving voice to these past pains and transgressions.

To further illuminate the significance of this, Pluto takes ~ 248 years to complete a cycle through the zodiac. Because it moves so slowly, many people never experience the transit that you are about to complete. If people do experience Pluto-Sun conjunctions as you have, it never repeats. It feels so important to highlight this because it means that you are walking now with very unique medicine. From an astrological perspective - you've gone through the underworld portal, and while yes, there is no finite endpoint to our evolution — you're fully completing something very significant - and are emerging with more vision, awareness, presence, skills to navigate hardship, and deeper contact with the real humanity of our feeling selves."

This is a little back story and a description of a most profound change in my mental health.

I didn't have a great storybook childhood. My parents were just below the poverty line. My father was a Junior High School (the school that I would attend) janitor, and my mother worked in the kitchen. Sometimes, we'd eat five-pound cans of government-issued green beans. They didn't have a lot of money. I was the last child of four, and six years separated my older sister from me, and she hated me. Really hated me. She would choke me on the floor until I couldn't breathe. I can't wear a turtle neck to this day. She held me upside down at the top of a Ferris wheel when I was 6 and screamed we're all gonna die. She'd break something and tell my mother it was me; then I'd get beaten. I'm not terribly sure of how much physical abuse there was, but I remember many incidents.

My sister was the bad seed. At fourteen, she ran away from home to California, and my mother went to get her. At fifteen, she stole their credit card and went again, and they went and got her. At sixteen, she did it again, this time getting pregnant, my mother went and got her. At seventeen, she had the same story, this time getting pregnant again and getting married to a man who beat her. At eighteen, she moved back to our house with two babies.

Whenever she would be brought home from California, I would lose my room. We lived in a very small three-bedroom, one-bath. When it got to the point of having a baby in my tiny room, I moved my bed into the closet and slept there for four years...true.

I was a good kid. I had a part-time job at a gas station at 12, and at 13, I got an after-school job cleaning classrooms after school. I bought my own clothes at age twelve. I was a good student. At fifteen, my guidance counselor called my parents and said if I took summer school, I could graduate, and they would get me into the University of Illinois on a full scholarship. My parents' response was "he was not special. If his brothers and sisters had to go through four years of high school, so does he."

I gave up. I only had three classes, and then I could go to my job packing boxes with medical supplies. I started at noon and worked till five. My grades went down because I didn't see any hope for my life except being a janitor.

Kids had teased me about being mushmouth's kid (my janitor dad didn't wear his dentures), and in my mind, I became that. I was one of two of my graduating high school class students who didn't go to college; the other guy went to jail. I drifted through various odd jobs to make money for guitars and such. I had been playing guitar about three hours a day since I was thirteen, mostly in a dark, unfinished basement.

I moved out on my nineteenth birthday into a friend's apartment. My mother gave me a cake and a twelve-page letter that said, "Don't ruin the family name, don't get arrested, don't get anybody pregnant (I was a virgin until I was eighteen)…twelve pages of hate followed, no love at all. I read it, and twenty minutes later, I was drunk for the first time in my life. I carried the janitor's kid and my mother's meanness around with me for fifty-three years, the same amount of time I had perfected drinking.

11-18 Dream from Journal

Dream Richard is sitting in his backyard at 3 am when an incredible black force descends upon the center of my field of vision.

It was the most awful feeling, and I woke up disturbed; I couldn't talk until after I had a shower. While I was in the shower, I realized the darkness was my mother. The letter she had written to me on my nineteenth birthday had been about her guilt. Her pain was so intense that she had to place that guilt on me. This letter was about my sister, not about me. I knew I had been a good kid - I was president of my church youth group, for heaven's sake, as a junior. I was a good kid, and the letter I had carried with me and the janitor's kid all those years just disappeared.

I was stunned at the depth of the realization and the witness of my acceptance. I accepted it so quickly because it was the truth.

11-26 Dream from Journal

It is the third night in a row where I have seen this huge black box in my backyard. The box is over where we have some of Woody's ashes deposited and a jade stone marker for him. When Dream Richard got up to the box, I expected the blackness and his ashes to be connected, but I was wrong. I was throwing things out of the box franticly over my left shoulder; I was bent over, almost feet off the ground, just violently throwing these black globs away over my shoulder.

When I woke up, I felt as if I was still doing it.

Re-entry to my morning routine was difficult. I went into the backyard and stood in the dirt in the rain. It helped me feel much more normal.

It takes courage.

Dec. 2nd Taking action for change

I woke up this morning really disturbed. I followed my therapist's direction and, went out before daylight and stood in the dirt in my backyard. An amazing thing happened: after five minutes, I started to notice small birds in the trees. I could feel a slight wind, and my troubled mind dissolved into joy. I had found a tool that was working and is now part of my life.

Dec. 17 Diary entry

After a weekend of no power in our home, my emotions were pretty raw; rather than totally losing my mind, I incorporated my five words of Thoughtful, Aware, Present, Continuity, and Honor into my thoughts and daily walk. It certainly helps me keep my awareness that there is a bigger world out there than the tiny one I sometimes lock myself within.

Dec. 20 Dream from my journal

Last night, Dream Richard woke up in the closet I had slept in for 4 years. It wasn't scary, and it is further proof to me that I can travel in my dreams safely.

It did take me a long time to reintegrate back into my daily life; I did feel detached.

Continuity

I didn't know how to end this book. I went over several possibilities in my mind, but nothing stuck. Last night in my dreams, I dreamed how to bring this document to a conclusion, so this is the last chapter; I write this on 12-24-24. There is no end to this story; it will continue. It is continuity. Yes, Woody's physical presence is no longer, but I find that he is with me every day. My feelings about him aren't all about grief anymore; they are about awe, wonder, and gratitude. Awe, in the facts of what he taught me, what he let me see, and how he continues his lessons to me. Wonder and gratitude in the fact that I can't believe the changes that have occurred in me.

This year has been a roller coaster with no bottom. Every time I think it can't get worse, the ride goes faster, and it gets darker. In the past month, I've begun to see some light on the horizon. I not only have hope, but I know that I will learn to live my intent; *my intent every day is that I learn to live a more loving and richer life*.

I have lost the guilt and poor self-image that I carried with me for most of my life. It started with being bullied and teased in junior high school about my father (mushmouth) and my mother, who served meals in the kitchen. I understand that the hateful and guilt-packed letter that my mother gave me on my nineteenth birthday was not about me but about my evil sister and my mother's guilt. I have learned that I was a good kid, a lonely and directionless kid, but I was a good kid. This realization alone was worth the price of the ticket. It was worth the pain and the loss that I felt with Woody. Again I am grateful that he was the catalyst of this enormous change.

I know that the reason Woody was in my life was to be the catalyst for the profound change that has occurred in me, and for that, I will always be grateful and will continue to follow my new path.

I have learned and accepted the fact and responsibility that I am a dreamer. I woke up at 3:30 this morning with the clearest of minds. In that clarity, I obtained the knowledge that I am a gifted dreamer. I saw three distinct paths in dreams. The first path was that Dream Richard could travel and be quite active. That when I see myself in my dreams, I am truly there. Where I don't know, but I know there is a seam in the world that I am now allowed to inhabit. That I have the ability to call on Dream Richard when I am troubled.

The second path was that Dream Richard could call upon his allies, both known and unknown, for deeper understanding, no matter the subject.

And the third path is one of rest and deep sleep. Since losing Woody, my bed has been a battleground. My dreams were so upsetting that I would wake up and just sit in the dark and cry. The grief would be a burden that I didn't think I could bear. Now, if I wake up with that type of dream, it's off to the backyard, and some  time with my feet in the dirt or to sit quietly in the front room with Faith as she sleeps. She is a true gift.

So, instead of an ending, my journey will continue. If I can keep my intention to live a fuller, more loving life as my compass, I know that things will continue to improve and astound me. That I will grow in my understanding of how the universe works and how it relates to me. That Dream Richard will have some amazing adventures, and from those adventures, no matter how black, I will find amazing growth and understanding about myself and the world around me.

I can never show enough gratitude to the people who brought me through this: my wife Wendi, Dr. Eliot Light, and his staff, Dr. John Paul Beaudoin, and Ophilia Mandara.

And I want to honor and respect myself that. I took on such a journey with an open mind. I have never been able to say that I honored and respected myself before, an enormous mental and physical change. Thank you, Woody, your gifts keep on giving.

I don't know how this story ends, but one thing I know.

It takes courage.

Bios

Richard Newman

Richard is a filmmaker, music video producer, musician, and writer. He has written three books on photography. He is the producer-director of the award-winning documentary *Addicted to Joy*. He has taught for the *Santa Fe Workshops* and the *Calumet Institute*. He has lectured in Germany, England, Australia, New York, Los Angeles, San Francisco, Chicago, and Boston. He writes a bi-monthly blog on Substack.com, *Wood Water Soul*. Married to Wendi for over forty years, he is a devoted dog Dad to Faith.

Wendi Newman, BSc, CDBC, CPDT-KA

Wendi is a certified dog behavior consultant with many years of advanced training in animal behavior. She works with dogs suffering from a variety of behavior issues, but her specialty is reactivity and aggression. She has a deep love and respect for dogs and their intelligence, adaptability, and sensitivity to humans. Wendi is also a professional writer and publishes a newsletter, *Raising Faith*, on Substack.com. In her spare time, you'll find Wendi studying behavior science and protocols, growing orchids, and enjoying time on the beach with her husband, Richard, and their dogs.

Ophilia Mandara

Ophilia Mandara is a multidisciplinary creator, educator, facilitator, and lifelong devotee of the creative and mystical arts. She is an initiate in the Dagara lineage of ancestral divination, has studied and practiced astrology for over twenty years, and is a certified Embodied Imagination® dreamwork practitioner. Whether through visual, musical, or spiritual channels, Ophilia is moved to help her clients and audience reconnect with their innate wisdom, inspiration, and sense of belonging. Find her, her music, and her offerings at www.planetarybloom.com.

www.ingramcontent.com/pod-product-compliance
Lightning Source LLC
Chambersburg PA
CBHW051219120626
46547CB00013B/1425